Endorsements for *Or: An Autobiography*

'Haunted thick and variously', *Or: An Autobiography* stages a non-binary, verbicovisual encounter with Virginia Woolf's modernist 'biography', *Orlando* and its kin, in the form of a collaged and shaped assemblage, a ghostly bag of 'queer tricks'. Arranged in chapters with bifurcated pages, *Or* makes its own place in the tide of 'documents, both private and historical', as Woolf had it, with fluency, invention, candour and verve. Experimental sonnet sequence above, auto-biblio-biographical essay below, each a fragmentary, bookish constellation of green, gender, sex, submission, love, wind, water, flowers, trees and centaurs, complete with addended textual apparatus. *Or* takes Toby Fitch's evolving work in visual and citational poetics in a new direction that is self-reflexive, scholarly, intimate and touching.

Kate Lilley

Or: An Autobiography is a pleasure to read and reread, with an ebb and flow that's cyclical, amorphous and gloriously ambiguous. *Or* resurrects and honours *Orlando* with playful care and genderfuckery, while revealing and refracting the work back on itself. This is a book of multitudes, resisting resolution and posing as many questions as it answers.

Rae White

Toby Fitch in *Or: An Autobiography* offers us a virtuosic reshaping grammar, an or-ness, that challenges the stereotyping of his/their/our bodies, their genders and physical forms, their phases and exchanges. This is a brave work, vulnerable and ambitious, intimate yet expansive, lucid, satiric and frisky, as it shapeshifts across the page, making short shrift of expected poetic and gender modalities: poem/prose, line/sentence, collage/memoir, top/bottom, either/or/both? It's 'a wild experiment', embracing language's transformative power, its enthusiasms, its wardrobe of trickery, its incongruities and revelations, its erotics and its tenderness.

Jill Jones

Or

Toby Fitch

Born in London and raised on unceded Gadigal land, Toby Fitch is a Senior Lecturer in Creative Writing at the University of Sydney and the author of various collections of poetry, including *Sydney Spleen* (2021) and *Where Only the Sky had Hung Before* (2019). Toby lives in Sydney's inner west with his partner and their three children.

Also by Toby Fitch

Everyday Static (Rare Objects #52 chapbook, Vagabond Press 2010)
Rawshock (Puncher & Wattmann 2012)
Quarrels (chapbook, Stale Objects dePress 2013)
Jerilderies (Vagabond Press 2014)
The Bloomin' Notions of Other & Beau (Vagabond Press 2016)
Undulating Cloud Sonnet (chapbook, Stale Objects dePress 2017)
Born to Creep (chapbook, Stale Objects dePress 2018)
ILL LIT POP (Cerberus Press / Flying Islands 2018)
Where Only the Sky had Hung Before (Vagabond Press 2019)
Object Permanence: Selected Calligrammes (Penteract Press 2019)
Sydney Spleen (Giramondo Publishing 2021)
Object Permanence: Calligrammes (Puncher & Wattmann 2022)

Toby Fitch

Or

An Autobiography

UPSWELL

First published in Australia in 2026
by Upswell Publishing
Perth, Western Australia
upswellpublishing.com

Upswell operates in the city of Perth, on ancient country of the Whadjuk people of the Noongar nation who remain the spiritual and cultural custodians of this beautiful land. We acknowledge their continuing connection to country and express gratitude to elders past and present for their strength and creativity...Always was, always will be, Aboriginal land.

ISBN: 978-1-7642397-0-7

NATIONAL LIBRARY OF AUSTRALIA

A catalogue record for this book is available from the National Library of Australia

Cover design by Chil3, Fremantle
Typeset in Foundry Origin by Lasertype
Printed by Lightning Source

To be, or not to be, that is the question

William Shakespeare

Never to be yourself and yet always—that is the problem

Virginia Woolf

Contents

A Note of Explanation, or A Little Introductory Tale of Bemusements and Disenchantment with the Queen

Once upon a time there was a marvellously made Or,
a blue-and-white, marble-malachite,
hot-cold water-at-will,

a because-they-didn't-live-in-London-anymore-rabbit-hole-
which-nobody-had-ever-seen
sort-of ghost. Haunted thick and variously

by vows of love, by songs (where they survive unbroken)
sung (out of a happy heart perhaps),
Or was an inquisitive spirit

up to date in fact. Other people were not
in their turn able to
do trees, enchanting things. Moreover,

peer into the Or Tree as they might in consideration
of their shilling, being greedy, there were some
could never see (though everybody

knows children see), nor make. Genius
(being in the moment in company under circumstances)
would have made of Or a conspicuous beanstalk

waved off to the ball, but, worn as a locket
they were the pea who had given the Princess
such a sleepless night,

had been present at the death of Bluebeard
so naturally it was only to be expected. Built for the Queen
of England (it was not in keeping with the rest

of their principles) they prided
themself on following the fashion of the abandoned
Or Tree. They were able to return to Europe,

to the fashions prevalent
among silk, hair, and nightingale,
banished as an artificial bird as they were.

In the twenties of the twenty-first century in two minds
and short skirts, Or found themself
brilliant, greatly delighted by their own dark

listening to the stories of Boccaccio and his friends
in a villa above Florence, way back (this
was one of their new expressions)

in the fourteenth century. They amused themself
by sleeping every night
in a different amusement perk,

obliged to discover a few disasters fully
dressed about their ears. Stuck between two floors
of pleasure, it must be remembered that

all modern inventions were new in the past
and sorely perplexed Or
(and Aladdin), every morning

going off, bed disarranged,
blinds quite sure they could furnish any love
having puzzled through a dirty joke. But now, of course,

Or bethought themself (and the books
in the library) the matter made
and the enigma which will once and for all be.

The Or Tree

Chapter 1

For no-doubt sex in fields
of asphodel—fields watered
by strange rivers—Or would
steal away from mother and the cocks
grinned at them through shrunken lips.
Skull so vast that there seemed trapped
the wind itself, Or's face threw the window open
to the height of their desire. Eyes came out
of the northern mists wearing leopard.
Like butterfly wings deciphering
drenched violets, the water
brimmed in Or,
widened
them.

I'm on the green sheets of our bed, with my partner F and our eldest child E. I've been talking with F for some years about identifying, maybe, as non-binary, but these have been private conversations, so it's a bit of a surprise when E not only comes out casually as 'they', but then goes on to ask me—pointedly, like they'd always known—'Would you prefer to be classified as "they", Daddy?' Maybe. I don't know. Maybe I'd prefer to

Disturbed, Or
turned to walk out
and dipped,
describing,
as all young poets
are forever describing
in order to match it,
the shade of green.
Green in nature
is one thing,
in literature
another precisely—
bring them together and
they tear each other to pieces.

---

be declassified completely. Or reclassified as … green, for example. Green can mean all kinds of things, emotionally, psychologically, spiritually. ('Green things are flowers too'. Frank O'Hara.) But can it stand in for the multiplicity I am, the fluidity I'd like to embody? ('[C]ould I lose myself in this abstraction[?]' Romaine Brooks.) Some memories are green. I once wrote a few Sapphic stanzas about that:

A trifle clumsy (clumsiness
often mates with
love of solitude), Or naturally loved
solitary places, vast views
and to feel ever and ever uphill
through ferns, startling deer, wild birds
—the English Channel, wave
upon wave of pleasure
gliding with puffs of smoke
from which came the flung self
on earth—it was anything
so long as it was hard, a heart
that tugged, a heart filled with
spiced and amorous gales.

'When I was a child I played alone below / silver helicopter leaves that autumn spun, / no wind, down on to my skin and the toys I / buried in the green. // When bigger boys would bully me for being / a girl I'd stare into the dead seas of their / eyes, stick a real gumnut up my nose and not / speak to anyone. // Now here I am making all kinds of weird shapes / of words to animate my whirling feelings / and anchor them to the beauty

Pale clouds hung
from little leaves, limbs grew
heavy on the ground as if all the
fertility activity of the summer eve
were woven web-like
about their body. White
clouds turned red,
woods purple, valleys
black. A trumpet
reduplicated
itself, darkness
pierced
with
lights —

---

of the world's / waves. O how it waves!' I'm thinking partly of trees in the wind: watching their leaves undulate, I'm stricken by the vertigo of meaning. Trees and their limbs have always been my favourite things to draw, centred in a landscape of flowers, mountains, river and moon. At age 7, among the leathery green leaves of bush lilies and bright heads of birds of paradise in our front garden, I imagined I was She-Ra, not

Or tore up the winding staircase,
tossed their stockings to one side,
jerkin to the other. No less than six inches,
a double dahlia was in front of them
like a dirty thought, a pen—their eyes
globed and clouded like some green stone
of curious texture. Was this a poet
who sees ogres, satyrs, perhaps
the depths of the sea
(head in a bowl of water)—
a great queen with thin hands
and long fingers always curling—
a body strung together
by a thousand fears?

He-Man, and wore Mum's tights to fight an imaginary Skeletor, climbing the pale pink mountain of our house. The 50-odd winding front steps were a river when it rained. ('When you see your reflection in water, do you recognise the water in you?' Roni Horn.) I don't know whether you've had this experience, but when I'm watching water I hear snippets from books drifting up from the ripples: '... a way a lone a last a loved a

Eyes flashed yellow in the water.
Or slept without knowing it.
For women's hearts, green in mind,
Or had written a score
of intricate sonnets
which had the look of innocence:
eyes, mouth, nose, breast, hips
and hands—the youth became them.
Strength, grace, romance, folly—
poetry rang among the cushions'
boyish memory of cheeks.
Lined with frost, a dyed
river ran sluggishly
full of shadows.

---

long the / riverrun, past Eve and Adam's, from swerve of shore to bend of bay, brings us by a commodius vicus of recirculation back to ...' (James Joyce). These bottom-of-the-page passages were originally modelled on the footnotes in Roni Horn's *Another Water*, cyclical fragments about water beneath her large close-up photographs of the surface of the River Thames (in London, where I was born), a surface

The mirror—brazen hussy—
saw Or kissing the mirror
and crashed, wore man's
treachery to an end.
Or was the weather itself,
auroral. Lingering
twilights blazed,
translating
withered ambiguities.
Our doubtful age
(the age of self)
kept blooming
and fading
as short flowers.

---

that is rippling, multiple and mutable, unsettled and unsettling, and which stands in implicitly for the indeterminacy of an androgynous identity. I added footnotes to my poem, jagging from the slippery shapes above, but they turned into vectors, aimed like jets of urine at flowers. So I've chosen instead this fragmentary proto-essayistic format, hoping that it 'functions to place the viewer [reader] in relation to the images

Or's nature
dissed what name was,
plucked rhymes for them all in turn.
Or's taste was for the weed laid bare
rudely, and for the sympathy of blood.
Cheek seemed fresher, full of beer and stars.
Their arms coloured their songs
with hard acquisitive beaks.
Or was astir, ragged of hair
—gossip had seen them sleeping,
while their loves had been active
among the rubes and laden in the
eternal snows of
Or's poetry.

[text/poem] in a way that emphasises the experience of excess.' (Horn.) Hoping also that the particulars in these passages placed at the bottom, like roots, flow back up to the limbs and leaves of the poem above ('... the self that writes itself into existence.' McKenzie Wark.) I originally wrote this poem in stanzas of six lines, as Orlando apparently wrote 'The Oak Tree' (though Virginia Woolf never quotes from it), but I

Phantom fruit, their illicit
modern shame went not in quest
of 'reality'. Underlinen drew back,
was so ill of silk
and justice.
Within an inch of its life,
Or's window turned inward
to perverse, to flame trees deeply rooted
with phlegmatic sets of teeth.
White care lawyers came
to curry favour with the citizens,
birds froze in mid-air,
were seen to turn
visibly to powder.

---

decided that amorphous, ambiguously shaped sonnets flowing into and out of each other like waves, or kissing and caressing like petals or leaves, were more in keeping with Or's style, Or's indeterminacy. And (or) mine. ('And really, no matter how public the art, the speech act, no matter how many people are gathered around … aren't we at our core just speaking to one person?' T Fleischmann.) Or to the river of one's

The river was frozen to a depth of
six or seven miles,
was swept, decorated, and given all the semblance
of a pleasure ground with arbours, alleys
and drinking mazes.
Etcetera lovers dallied in showers,
balloons hovered motionless in the ice
of singular transparency, eels puzzled—
the river wrecked the person,
whatever name or sex,
whether fashioned entirely
in oyster-coloured velvet or trimmed
with some unfamiliar green-coloured fur. Or!
obscure whole person—

---

life? ('Can the river dissolve your identity just lying next to it, lying nearby and watching it?' Horn.) I've often felt my self to be as changeable as the weather (meaning the water inside me?), yet it's always somehow there, returning cyclical as a satellite—orbiting what? ('What cannot be named or confirmed with satisfaction exceeds every apparently satisfying act of nomination.' Judith Butler.) What if it was, or was like, a melon,

a pineapple,

an olive tree

a fox in the snow—

all in a derangement of the senses.

Senses were simple they were

at the same time extremely

out of the question—

for Or's own sex that is,

or was.

Fished from the bottom

Or turned hot, cold,

longed to hurl, to toss

with the beech trees and oaks.

---

a tree? Could a tree dissolve your identity if you stood next to it long enough, waving to it in the wind? Or would you have to climb it, entwine yourself in its limbs, to glimpse the stars behind clouds? Occasionally when I'm watching the moving leaves I hear them whispering snippets of poems: 'Those stars, that glide behind them or between, / Now sparkling, now bedimmed' (Samuel Taylor Coleridge). My stars tell me

It was through this
red-cheeked accident
that Or spread
under the entertainment of
a laughable predicament,
tongue *dans le ravissement,*
mouth yawning sawdust
and cinders
and stuffed peacocks.
Ice turned to wine
Or's landscape—
manhood in deep water,
their most impassioned sonnets
blushed deeply in the world.

---

that, as a Sagittarian, I'm a centaur, a hybrid. The other day I saw a tree—not a cloud as you might expect, but a tree—that looked like a centaur, and like me! ('I won't talk about how water is a mirror. At night, the darkness of the water reflects the darkness of the sky. But when daylight comes again the water will remain dark, cutting everything in it off from everything beyond it.' Horn.) I have a complex relationship

Drollery answered
in perfect French,
the subject changing
from a sulky stripling
to a dancebeat. Or's
sapphire left hand stung it
in its tenderest part—
the public part of the river
where dogs ran six abreast
all day long. Rebel head
took to the city. Where they had
the river to themself they lay
lulled in a swoon,
cindery.

---

with my sex. At age 4, I could piss for metres into the air, but it was painful, because my urethra was tight—I needed an operation to free it from its strictures. While I was recovering, my parents had to pin me to the bathroom floor to insert a healing cream into my cock's eye to prevent infection. I didn't really have good sex until at least age 21. It took excessive patience from others and trust from me to work out how

Laughing, Or would fall
suddenly into moods—
'All ends in death'—
extravagant words.
Nothing thicker than a knife's blade
separates happiness from melancholy.
Snow, cream, marble,
cherries, alabaster—
none of these like fox, like waves
(when you look down on them from a height),
like emerald, like sun—so ransack the
language, failed landscape,
another tongue too frank,
sun imprisoned in a hill.

---

to make this at once emotionally sensitive and slightly physically desensitised 'male' organ work. ('The thing about shame is that it eats at you until it fully consumes you. Then you cannot tell the difference between their shame and your own—between a body and an apology.' Alok Vaid-Menon.) Perhaps that's why, emotionally, I think of myself as a bottom, like water settling into negative space, though I also love

Remembering petticoats, Or ran
with the passion of a poet whose poetry is half
pressed out by pain, history, family—
ashamed, covered with the fur of all sexes,
doubt like quicksand in the lower parts of the ship.
Or wrapped in dreams all the hardships
true landscape cannot entice. Anxious tree-plant,
on the first dark night confident thoughts saw them
blotted out in a red cloud—Or was outraged
by the foulness of this tawny wide-cheeked monster.
It might have been the fault of the consonants—
pink, tallow, rank, their breast hooked by a great fish
and rushed through the waters unwillingly yet
with consent and against all red sunsets.

---

twirling about like a top—as in the poems above, or when dancing with F and our kids. ('A kissed mouth doesn't lose its fortune; on the contrary it renews itself just as the moon does.' Giovanni Boccaccio.) Hence the diversatility of trees: each singularity formed by the ebb and flow of organisms is also a multiplicity informed by larger familial units—copses, forests, ecosystems. Or is that just me dreaming? If 'the opacity

A grove of trees
with bulbs
for leaves
were lit. All the west
seemed fancy again—
perpetually white,
gulls circling, a million globes
translating all the red of Or's cheeks—
yet night came on like a grey skeleton.
Everything suffered emaciation
and transformation. A deep
note struck on a tuning fork
boomed hither and thither
on the surface of a river.

---

of the world dissipates in water' (Horn), it also dissipates in dreams. Recently I dreamt I was scaling a grass hill to a music festival, whose entrance was through some huge clear sheeting shaped like a dome. On the inside were just two people, an old school friend I no longer talk to and a newer friend, a trans friend from university, playing frisbee. Hard and fluoro green, it was excellent for throwing long distances. I tried to

Above
and around this
brilliant circle like a bowl
of darkness pressed the deep black.
Then into this darkness there began to rise
flowering rockets, serpents. Or found a way
to end their privacy and encounter the sharp eyes
that were on the watch for them—catchers, scholars,
ostlers, citizens and, as always, trees. The haunted
press stood opposite like a Punch & Judy
show, and still the words stirred
like music in the beer—
even words without
meaning came to.

---

find a way in through the clear sheeting. There was a tight overlapping slit that seemed the only way in. I used my hands to prise it apart, but it was too tight for my angular body to squeeze through. I ran around the other side of the clear tent dome—the sun was white, the grass dewy—sliding my hand along the sheeting to feel for another slit. The next was just as difficult to manoeuvre through, but I levered my hunkering limbs

Or methinks should now have been a huge
eclipse of sun and moon, and that the affrighted
globe should yawn in their ear. Long before
midnight, however, Or was the night
so inky that a man was on you before
he could be seen at the rustle of a woman's
dress. The lights which burnt downstairs
were extinguished (negligence of
man before dawn, who would sit there
trolling till rolled asleep on sand).
The blow took a minute to realise that
these were raindrops—the hard sky poured
the self forth in one profuse fountain
steaming and droning and gleaming.

---

inside. I could hear our newer friend saying they'd thrown 30 from 30, and then they were facing me and hurling the frisbee in my direction. It landed comfortably in my hand. ('A fragment would seem to be … a broken-off part of a whole. Does it also imply, as with other broken-off pieces, that enough of them would make a whole, or remake some original whole, some ideal whole?' Lydia Davis.) My body still doesn't

Voices echoed in the leaves.
Doom was a sealed feeling heart
jangling subterraneously,
bitten by a swarm of snakes.
The tremendous rain sagged a little
at the knees. Immovable irony was
now a turbulent yellow freedom
as if a sulphur spring had risen
from volcanic regions, burst
the ice asunder with such
vehemence that it swept these
massy, turn-one-giddy fragments
into riot and confusion—strewn
with icebergs, fantastically twisted.

---

know how to let go, how to be inside, outside, and of itself all at once. ('What part of you did you have to destroy in order to survive in this world?' Vaid-Menon.) Do I write to rediscover that part? Growing up, I never realised I was dysphoric. I just kept twisting myself toward the light of others' expectations, like a tree, like a body of water. ('Water is sexy. (I want to swim in it—to move, song-like, through it. I want to

Many of Or's parts perished by their own
cupidity. Eyes were carried away
on icebergs with an extraordinary
amount of cooking utensils.
Or clapped, rounding a bend
of the river fast filling
with water. Or thought
the shape of a ship flinging—
self made in rage—
would breast the flood of sex.
Faithless, fickle—
the swirling waters
took their words,
their broken little feet.

---

swim in it—push, kick, thrash, slide myself through it. I want to swim in it. I want to be held by it.)' Horn.) I keep quoting Horn and can't not think about horniness, the desire to be one enough with your own body to let it touch and be touched—to connect with another body, F's body. ('Water is plural. How could it ever be singular?' Horn.) I want to be leaves in green waves.

we lay bare rudely,
in fields of asphodel,
web-like about
sex,
eyes like drenched violets, so larg
no doubt
in its tenderest part,
on the ice,
Or
slept all night
innocence
acquisitive beak
shade of gree
young poets are for eve
dans le ravissement.
an emerald, a fox
slenderly fashioned,
"All ends in death," Or

Chapter 2

Unenticed by dark religious systems
Or died for a week
(perambulating the house alone's
variety of skeletons of men,
we have to take death in small doses).
On the seventh day they woke at the usual time
with caterwauling in the chambers
of the brain, passed their hand across their brow
as if to wipe away some cloud, princess or ship—
the usual sedatives and irritants.
Memories that cripple life and animals
in great agony stirred moonlight
with a bat in the night's crypt
built upon corruption.

After drafting 'The Or Tree', it took me 7 years to come back to it, and much of that time was spent reckoning with my awkward relationship to gender. It took Orlando over 300 years to write 'The Oak Tree', in which time they lived through multiple eras, had affairs with a queen, poets and critics, and changed gender from man to woman. Not being this or that, I could keep redrafting this work all my life. ('If you prefer,

We that dance and sing must lie
beneath invention—
the cardinal labour of composition
of what a hand can do
clouded in trousers,
contorted with cogitations,
melancholy, indolence, passion.
With glow-worms, with a love of literature
infected by a germ
said to be bred of the pollen
of the asphodel eye, Or
evaporated. Reality is phantom
once the disease of reading the system
takes to writing.

/ I'll be pure raging meat, / or if you prefer, / as the sky changes tone, / I'll be absolutely tender, / not a man, but a cloud in trousers!' Vladimir Mayakovsky.) The number of times I've been asked if I'm gay, as if that would explain my effeminacy (to them; or force me to question it myself), would outnumber my years. ('Hence, I concluded that trouble is inevitable and the task, how best to make it, what best way to be in it.'

Deeply smitten in Or's hand
as if Ajax had lacked,
a great hole smelt of poems published,
was an inexpiable disgrace.
Fingered, The Or Tree quill
has already played many queer tricks
on us, making us so unequally
of clay and diamonds,
rainbow and granite, stuffed
into a case for the poet who delights
in muddle and mystery, who knows
why our daily movements
are like the passage of a ship
on an unknown sea-glass horizon.

Butler.) Can you hear that other poem drifting up from the waves? ('It feels like an unfinished / A body of water, potential to do so much, yet eventually bottled.' Travis Alabanza.) As an aside, I note the names of the boys who seemed to think calling me a girl would hurt: Paul, Oliver, Neil, Robert, James, Brendan et al. These names haunt me, but only when I think of how I withheld my emotions from them while they had less

Or, who has so much to answer for
besides the perhaps unwieldy length
of this sentence (memory is odd
disconnected fragments in a gale),
should have struck their pen in the big
bright eyes of the Poetry witch
and heart their dancing ground, but
to break the solitude of years and communicate
with the outer world, Or, in a state,
writ a book which outshone, which transfigured
Sir P__, Sir O__, Sir N__, Sir R__, Sir J__, Sir B__ et al.
A skull and the moonlight, in sheer abstraction,
were dust—The Or Tree
with its million leaves rose from the ashes.

---

trouble expressing theirs. ('Ethics requires us to risk ourselves precisely at moments of unknowingness, when what forms us diverges from what lies before us, when our willingness to become undone in relation to others constitutes our chance of becoming human.' Butler.) Once, aged 9, I felt I had so little control of those emotions, burning waves of them, that throughout the day—in class, in the shadier parts of the playground, on

In a small bag the poet slouched,
the dog had bit them. Mankind
was puzzled as to where
to place them—the Poet Stranger.
The sacred subject of poetry flashed green,
thumped glass. Jilted at nature (so rash as to write
a mouse truth) Or's great spleen burnt as ice.
Their unconscious spine was fireworks
inside a mattress of machinery
(think conspiracy / think against).
Poetry was dead—Shakespeare, Marlowe,
Jonson, Browne, Donne
could not think green laughs,
banking poetry in the pay cell.

---

the bus home—I repeatedly carved a uniform line with my thumbnail into the soft bit of skin on the inside of my right kneecap, until I sliced right through. ('Well, I was hidden from myself, hun.' Wark.) I kept slicing into it even as it bled, perhaps to affirm my own liquidity, but also to feel it burn. ('No one will ever know it and a sin that's hidden is half forgiven.' Boccaccio.) I have the scar to prove it. These days I write

Ill of lit, Or's experiments
loved the future life
of these doctrines—drunk silly things.
'Stap my vitals, Bill,' green explained,
trembling to be a poet, to brawl,
to go and say a thing like 'Glawr! Glawr! Glawr!'
Alone, they would lie in bed every morning
reading green—that's called Glawr.
Or abandoned all hope of discussing
their own work with green anecdote gods
and rather quarrelled with scribble—
poetry on bills that the rest of time
spent junketing in beer gardens—
green pitch mimicry.

---

to find something resembling a self in my poems, snipping and slicing them until a kind of topiary—a kind of Toby—emerges. ('... fragments to mimic the fissures of self'. Guignery and Drag.) After a falling out with poetaster Nick Greene over his parody of their poetry, Orlando burned their entire poetic oeuvre except 'The Oak Tree'. ('When a part of you is so heavily scrutinised and interrogated, in order to protect yourself you

A strange indefinite something good God
was so full of instruments
—a geranium, a carnation, an oak
—that oranges grew underground and trees
twittered at his jokes, all of which gave Or
a bitch of an apoplexy.
A slothful plaguey green spirit
came between the sheets and on the turf.
Weed, Or thought—green affection.
So splendid to make toasted cheese.
Green children had been baking mud pies
in gin—green-spirited satire,
doubt about green, green
with deadly composure.

---

have to present it as immutable.' Alabanza.) With that in mind, I cut and shaped my own poem, chapter by chapter, from the surviving fragments of a copy of *Orlando* I'd burned ritualistically in my back garden—or let's say in an imaginary garden where trees hush, trees laugh, trees bloom, trees stretch, trees rock, trees shiver, trees tear themselves apart and mirror themselves underground, their own roots communing with

Done with men, Literature was a farce.
Two things alone remained to trust—dogs
and a vast amount of illusion.
The Or Tree dreamed.
Secluded writing and reading saw young ferns
unfurl, the moon sickle, cobwebs bloom
and fade with amazing punctuality.
From the queer element of the human
came the strangest variety of selves,
and from a numbskull phantom brain,
from a parchment Hustler heart—books and lit
metaphors rushed, cumbered the bottom
of the sea grown about with bones
and dragonflies of the drowned.

---

others. ('With the ability to freely and knowingly become one or many of a limitless number of genders for any length of time, at any rate of change.' Kate Bornstein.) Do you notice the way these sentences puddled here reflect (on) the poem(s) above? ('The colour of water (whatever it is) changes constantly. Half of it is in the sky.' Horn.) Maybe you won't care for the topiary above. Maybe you'll put the book down, or look for

Another

\ metaphor, /

\ \ by / /

Jupiter! Manifestly untruthful, no dragonfly, unless

under

very exceptional circumstances, could live

/ / at \ \

/ the \

bottom

of

the

sea's

green

sky.

---

certainties down here. ('But there are more—more leaves, more roots: at the bottom of my brain, at the bottom of the sea.' Horn.) So let's change the subject. My dad's favourite insect is the dragonfly, as is mine. He and I have various ornaments decorated with dragonflies. My most treasured is a beige stone jewellery box with a large black dragonfly engraved on its lid (green in a certain light). I keep slips of paper in

The austere spirit of
poetry darkens like a flight of girls fleeing
the embraces of woods. We despaired of being able
to solve the problem of what poetry is, and what truth is
fell into deep profit,   tragedy. Blasted green!—poet
of immortality   in the bin! As to the value of
obscurity,   it struck Or anonymously
like a bullet   of rejected love which
has only seen thoughts,
some of them oblong.
A massive wall
curled into the air
never more
inhuman.

---

there—things my kids E and M have written to me. You can hear poems in their leavings: 'the girls ran along tonight's question mark … looming in the agate sky … pointing them toward dewdrops and tears' (John Ashbery). Once, in one of my poems, I permutated into a mermaid, thanks to E and M—though they, in their shift away from the gender F and I assigned them, seem to have abandoned mermaids lately. Are

Furnishing man, the odious parliament
made a stain on the carpet—
crimson, white, walnut, damask.
It is an effect that lists have upon us
—we are beginning to yawn.
There are sixty-five pages more and the total
sum now millions of fragments of our time—
silver, topaz, snow, crocus and rose,
magnolia, dahlia, hyacinth,
lily and aster, apple and cherry, pear, mulberry,
evergreen and blue dolphins with mermaids on their backs,
velvet and gilt: The Or Tree looked as if, in the process
of writing, it would be completely unwritten,
a fountain drained . . .

---

mermaids now too girly, too green, for them? Should I remind them of the innate slipperiness of being, of the potential merness in all of us, before they harden? ('I cast a shadow into myself, becoming myself. The shadows and dirt thicken my waters with a darkness and distance that slices through everything: identity, place, geology.' Horn.) Rainbow and granite. My skull feels weighted down by its overrated undergrowth of

... a shadow in riding hood,

a stranger twitching in the rain,

averse to his and hers. And so,

with the shapeliest legs,

Or unloved the argument

between the sexes.

Dark, and with coarse

black wings, love itself

wheeled about,

haunted Or every

day and night

—uninhabitable—

pelting them

with hazelnuts.

---

flesh, hair and skin. Am I still green, still slippery enough, to morph into waves I can't yet fathom? ('Other water rushes along in its unseeable depth and permeability, full of darkness that has no image.' Horn.) What tree is it that whispers then hushes overhead, undifferentiated from the dark in our back garden, full of night skies that have no answer? Not being this or that.

rainbow and granite,
bare rudely,
haunted by a great variety
tree, with its million leaves
in fields of
odd disconnected fragments
so full of queer
in inexpiable disgrace.
made a stain
not for pay but for Glawr."
slept all
attitudes of great agony
ed with a love of literature.
Of the nature of poetry itself, Or
shade of gree
dans le ravissement.
A skull; a finger.
"All ends in death," Or
perhaps unwieldy length of this sentence,
slenderly fashioned

Chapter 3

Regret played a part in Or's public life,
had a finger in some of the most delicate.
Revolution broke out,
paper was scorched.
We have done our best to piece out
a meagre summary from the charred
fragments that remain
but often it has been necessary
to heart bright
unseasonable flowers
and snuff the acrid, curled
and anointed, one after another,
into red boxes.
Only fragments flourish—

Here I am at the bottom again, among my many fragments: 'the decayed fragment (Sappho); the contemporary fragment (text messages, twitter, blog posts, etc.); the modernist fragment (T.S. Eliot; fragment as mark of psychological disintegration); Freud's fragment (dreams, slips, etc. as thruways to the unconscious); the sampled or plagiarized fragment; fragment as waste, excess, or garbage; the footnote; fragment as frame

of their contents we cannot
speak, can only testify that
Or was a seal—diversely purple—
preferred Constantinople,
their badness smoking a
hookah punctiliously.
Human sunk beneath the surfeit,
overtaken by the gloom of the poem
(no doubt a cloak manuscript),
their eye-green life forgotten
and without any
need to think—
they spoke in echo:
no attachments, no pelt.

(Degas, Manet); life narrative as fragment: we can't see the whole until we're dead, and then we can't see it (pathos); fragment as psychological terror (castration, King's head); fragment as fetish, or as 'organ-logic', as pornography; fragment as metonym and synecdoche; fragment as that which is preserved, or that which remains; fragment as the unfinished or the abandoned; and so on and so forth.' (Maggie Nelson.) To be

Here we pause among burnt papers
and little bits of tape full of holes,
some being quite illegible.
Somewhat long-winded,
rockets had come to
in the art of pyrotechny
with emotions of shame
observing sex and country.
A branch of the Judas tree had broken
the exact nature of pyramids of ice
from which black swans hang,
priceless, peaking with
fluency. People scarcely
know why.

---

submissive is also to be reactive, or to be ready to react, to moments of desire as others express them. ('Is this a ripple or a disturbance?' Horn.) These moments too are fragmented; leave you waiting, guessing, yearning. ('In an Arctic iceberg, in your drinking glass, in that drop of rain, on that frosty windowpane, in your eyes, and in every other microscopic, microcosmic part of you (and me) all waters converge.'

Proudly erect, Or
took the golden strawberry
from the skies. Disorder
fell upon the scene.
Nobody has known
exactly what took place later that night
in a cloak: muffled amid bedclothes
that were much tumbled,
Or slept with poetry in which frequent
mention was made of an Or Tree,
also various state papers
of far greater importance,
signed and witnessed. Yet still, Or
was infidel, deep rose.

Horn.) You become expert at being particulate, splashed about, at reshaping yourself to others' whims. It also means you're harder to pin down. Late at night in bed, with a fluoro green light carving through the blinds, is sometimes the only time to explore one's amorphousness, lose one's inhibitions. ('The room I entered was a dream of this room.' Ashbery.) ('To be undone by another is a primary necessity, an anguish,

No sign of life broke into Or's room, left them
touched by the gentlest zephyr, wafted them apart:
hair—an avalanche of the driven snow;
brow—a diadem of icicles burning;
eyes—pure stars;
face—sickle-shaped and half among the clouds.
Meanwhile the Truth, making gestures in vain,
pealed, stark naked. Curiosity peeped in and threw up
a garment like a towel at the naked form which unforch
fell short by several inches.
The change of sex, though it altered their future,
did whatever to nothing the dark
drops fallen into clear pools
of complete surprise.

---

to be sure, but also a chance—to be addressed, claimed, bound to what is not me, but also to be moved, to be prompted to act, to address myself elsewhere, and so to vacate the self-sufficient "I" as a kind of possession.' Butler.) Am I me, are you you, are they them, who perform themselves in these moments? ('Who are you, Face, you who I am, whom I follow, you who look at me without seeing me, you whom I see without knowing

But let other pens treat of sex and sexuality—we quit,
indifferently. Much signs.
So perturbation. Such poesy.
In the giant tree shadow Or swung
too well pleased with the change to spoil it
by thinking—the whole camp egg and a pipe
must have been in secret commune
before the revolution of themselves, their science
of stealing and bird-snaring.
A sunset was blazing over the word 'beautiful'
—young men and women grazing, sky good to eat.
Elders became suss of the far wrong.
Or likened the hills to breasts, flowers to enamel, turf to rugs.
Trees were shags, sheep were everything.

---

whom, you in whom I look at myself, you who would not be without me, you whom I envelop, you who seduce me and into whom I do not enter, who are you, who is this being promised subjected to my gaze, to my objective, this being docile to my law, and who remains totally impenetrable for me? What is you? Who am I, you?' Hélène Cixous.) Suddenly I'm 10 years old again, lying on cut grass, gazing up into pines

Every-
thing in fact was eyeballs,
something found to be an imperfect
communication—looking for looking's sake.
Interpreting this to mean inky beauty
and the conceit of blank spaces, The Or Tree
became suspicious of the gaze, because Or is
someone who doubts, who sees their own great
rage as something broke, something to be cut
up into savage pearls questioning England,
centuries of ancient speak ('The whole Earth
is ours!'), which snatched land and
money and brought us
gentlemen.

---

after chasing my first real sexual crush for an hour around the school hall—a boyish teenage girl with long thick hair—feeling for the first time the green sting of unmet desire. ('Nature held me close and seemed to find no fault with me.' Leslie Feinberg.) Then, much later—while writing this poem—I stumble across an edition of *Orlando* whose cover shows a self-portrait by Romaine Brooks, *At the Seaside* (1914), which

No passion is stronger in the breast of 'man'
than the desire to make others fill with rage—
Liberal and Labor party moralities
dull as ditch water.
Or prefers a sunset, patterns of fig leaves.
Suddenly, a shadow—a green hollow—
deepened. The whole
landscape was
covered, marked with violet snow.
All was so clear and minute that
worms in the snow burst into a
passion of tears—breaking off,
their pearly embraces
were sincere.

---

looks uncannily like me (extra windswept). Most of her portraits are of women in masculine dress, imbued with melancholy, as if newly recoiled into themselves after a night in bed with another. I show the painting to F, who suggests I use it in a poem or collage. Could I undo myself with this abstraction? There I go, off to the top again, as if to shore up my fragments.

were sincere
Suddenly a shadow
haunted by a
since the world began
of sex and sexuality; we quit
of the driven snow;
rainbow and granite,
rudely,
But let other
sky good to eat, indeed!
threw a garment like a towel at the naked form
unfortunately, fell short by
violet shadows deepened
odd, disconnected fragments
not for pay but for Glawr."
slept all
attitudes of great agony
shade of gree
dans le ravissement.
natural sympathy which is between the se
whatever to alter their identity.
can be worn indifferently by either sex;
A skull,
slenderly
soon the whole
in death," Or
completely unwritten. For it is
unwieldy length of this sentence,

Chapter 4

It was a strange fact, sex
being minute in length under awning,
and skirts are fearful things to have
about one's heels. About to be deflowered
the loveliest in the world swim
in clothes like they're protection.
Ah! dark garments of the world,
a gloom (the obscurity which divides
the sexes in falsity) fell over roundabouts
exquisitely apparelled by hair. Dressing
and lacing so violently, Or thought
what an odd pass we have come to
prance, mincing out the words
to form the other.

At age 15, I was envious of the new boy who wore a kilt almost every day to school. He called me 'Bill', from Tobillius, an abbreviation I hated for how masc it was, but loved for the way it gave me licence to be otherwise, to be less classifiable, a cloud in fact. ('Every good biographer detests that riot and confusion of passions and emotions. Our simple duty is to state the facts as far as they are known, and so let the reader

Sex seemed to vacillate.
A delicious tremor in the cockpit.
It was a most whirligig state of mind to be utterly
blown, as in a million blue dolphins
twisting you to death.
Proud to remain abstract flesh and blood,
Or was so rapt at ear
when a man's voice said, 'Permit me Ma'am'
(and would happily have been hard
boiled within as the tulips were abloom
and the bees buzzing off giant resolute cliffs
were murmuring, 'How august, how
sublime, how . . .')—however,
coupling selves together felt culpable, strange.

---

make of them what they may.' Woolf.) Between 18 and 22, I had long thick curly hair. On a road trip around France with my godfather I was frequently referred to by strangers as 'madame', which, somewhere in my waters, I liked, though I didn't admit that, or know how to admit it, or who to admit it to. During the boy-who-wore-a-kilt's first few weeks, I said to him one day, naively and without context, as we walked

Twitchetting
thought spread round
like the turbulent waters
below a risen moon. Where the
poem might have been booming
nothing from bank to bank,
a parliament of watercraft was
error-stricken. Citizens took snuff
at street corners—rapid stuff.
A great number of decent citizens
humped, shadows slanting.
Smoking in the pot-pourri
of tired joy, Or's faith
could detect a stain.

---

down the long asphalt path to the basketball courts, 'I know how you feel.' To which he replied, 'You have no idea how I feel.' And of course I didn't know the details of his personal life, his family background, what particular riot and confusion he was feeling. But part of me still knows I knew something, even if it was diffracted through 'me'. Is this what Butler designates a 'gender uncertainty'? ('Every word that gets

Or, who was more ready to die than other people,
and moved by the humane jumble of them all
—the hair, the pastry, the blood, the tobacco—
reflected: they were a serpent of The Or Tree
believing that poetry can adulterate and destroy
more surely than lust or tolerance.
'Wicked world, I am losing my illusions
perhaps to acquire new legs—no, syllables!
—along a tumultuous avenue of self.'
Lips opened something intricate
and many-chambered within. Fabrication
went down like shadows, left a naked sky
twinkling in the damp phantasmagoria
of a disassemblable moment.

---

set down, every decision made—form, content, sentence structure, image—begins to define a work that previously was a kind of infinitely indeterminate mental cloud, or beautifully diffuse physical sensation.' Nelson.) I once dreamed I had no penis, just a curved section of nothing between my legs, like a Barbie, or like the 'Porsche bonnet' my brother poked fun at (self-consciously) when describing men with no

Overcome by the smell of some old ascetic
bewildered imprint—'By my life! The Or Tree!'—
Or, gentle creature pressing a cordial to their lips,
acted the part for ten minutes with great vigour
and then fell into the future: the pink perfection
of sex interspersed with tee-hees and haw-haws
of the strangest, highly ridiculous and grouse love.
Man should be shocked when men display emotion
—so shocked that Or came on Wednesday,
came on Thursday, came on Friday.
At wit's end Or came on Or, who was
half hiding their yawn—a simple device
to divorce the self, the lump of sugar
(the necessity of marriage voided).

---

pronounced bump in their pants. ('When I was young I decided that my sex, my gender, was nobody's business.' Horn.) I often wish I could be more bodily expressive. Not so that my orgasms are less of an emotional outpouring, but so that I can love my body, be comfortable in the love another has for my body, while loving their body too. My relationship with my own sexuality, as with gender, is also awkward—from late

Watching the many hundred flies at this game,
still awkward in the arts of sex—
no better method than this blue-bottled,
gently pressed, dumb-gazing at the ceiling
coloured scarlet.
Life and a lover,
Life and a lover,
life as green water
twittering erect in neat black knickerbockers
came and rang the bell. Or hid their manuscripts
and drove to safety—altogether brain.
Vain trifles they seem, clothes
have more important offices. Thus,
there is much to support our hearts.

Middle English (in the sense 'the wrong way round, upside down'): from dialect *awk*, 'backwards, perverse, clumsy' (from Old Norse *afugr*, 'turned the wrong way'). From 13 to 15, my nipples, or at least the glands beneath them, became so swollen I thought I might be growing breasts—maybe, despite my inevitable masculinity, I was growing them—and, perhaps out of a sense of conformity (or obligation) to my

Different though the sexes are, they intermix—
in every human being a vacillation—
the clothes they keep, the odd effect
it had in the particular case
of Or's curious mix.
Dress random?
shabby? formal?
power? tender?
donkey-beaten?
kitten-drowned?
At dawn, one suit
beyond the powers of the
truth, they did drink with burst
tears, found mathematics rattling on the cobbles.

---

supposed emerging manhood, I spent a lot of mental energy willing them to subside, sometimes even pressing them down to hold them in place as though they were buttons on a straitjacket threatening to burst open. Looking back, I wonder why I confided all this, or felt that it was something I needed to confide, in my mum, though her response, which might have been both tongue-in-cheek and deadly serious, now makes

F-
ashion
was fast deser-
ting that end of town:
'Lawk, if it ain't a mob of
stars crowding the heroin gravely.'
Yet in good reptile temper Or racked up
memory. Home at three or four in the morn,
cheeks like a Christmas tree and eyes like tar, take-
away was insipid. Society said nothing. Or was intense,
blazing south into bed, pitching and tossing monsters that
not even poets can deal with alone (either sex did not include the
management of a thousand etceteras and Or was apt to think of poetry
a little too much).

---

perfect sense: 'Toby Twirl, maybe you're turning into a girl.' Maybe I was. Maybe I was both boy and girl for a time. Maybe neither. My fear of ambiguity was certainly stronger than my fear of manhood. Or maybe it was a fear of duality. ('The deserts of our future will be deserts of water.' Horn.) That said, whenever a dress-up opportunity arises, my first instinct is always drag. I rarely go through with it, for fear of

In a miasma—'What the
devil is the matter with me dawn sky
bursting into tears and intercourse?'—
they would wag their front part,
elevate their hind,
jump, bark and slobber,
all sorts of artifice of their own quarrel
with Addison, Dryden, Pope,
the usual divinities,
these great men who chimed like credit.
Or doubted from the deck
of their ship the nature of their vision
being the antechamber to the busts of genius
in a niche in the wall.

---

provoking conversations about my wavery gender. The parodic element of drag lays gender open to possible renovation, but it also means sending up loved ones' sometimes immutable sense of sex and gender. It's one thing to do parody in literature, another in the flesh. F has always supported my fluid poetry, while I've often sucked the life out of a good moment with a few choice contrarian words, as many poets do.

With great trepidation
Or entered a dark semicircle, said
no more than three witty things.
The violets lay low. Or feared a cat dream.
Under a sofa they slunk, misshapen
by a variety of emotion darts—
malice, rage, triumph, wit, terror—
burning topaz emotions.
For if it is rash to walk into a rash,
it is still more rash to go home alone with a poet
who can destroy what atmosphere is.
Or should have been a heap of cinders
in the narrative. The less we see the more we
believe that the stars are rootled in darkness.

But when she instigated a conversation about (my) gender, 'I just looked at her and suddenly I felt things well up in me I thought I had buried' (Fleischmann). I've tried to bury myself in these notes—these passages through my understorey—so deeply and evasively that their ambiguous turns, juxtaposed or flowing into one another, make up a system of roots, or tributaries, that could be rearranged, just as the topiarian shapes

What an age! that the lynx casts off its skin
and the swan pays contributions to the embellishment
of an open enemy, pimping, splenetic, violent—man.
But the most important part of style—which is the natural
run of the voice in speaking, not green but born of the air
—breaks like a wave on bank notes, on commodity verses
all crumpled up. Future ages are extremely uneasy, scarcely
have room to breathe. Let us enjoy the immunity of any sex!
Leave it to the gentlemen to prove that this is impossible
in ill-lit, ill-paved, ill-ventilated times (it is he who is said
to have written the poems that were really hers).
Meanwhile, sustaining the different parts of doubt,
Or's petticoat joyed the love of an ambiguous turn
—a flower wasting hourly.

---

above are landmarks of relation, or stars in constellation, that could be rearranged into other constellations. Perhaps as you are reading either, some kind of wave-particle duality might emerge—a performance of the ambiguity of my gender and/or a confession of its latency. These and/or instincts aren't unusual, but they're seldom acknowledged as natural, and their suppression can result in ruptures of expression (poetry as a

No nearer consummation, night finally came—
junket naked on a balcony, shadows
on the blind drinking tea,
the stars in deep pits of stagnant water.
In the middle of the streets, poetry and filth
swarmed all over the smell of them.
A hot small cloud gathered,
the cloud increased and spread
with extraordinary speed—the eastern sky,
the west and north moving above the city
engulfed by the twelfth stroke of midnight.
A turbulent welter of cloud,
the century of darkness was over,
the century of darkness had begun.

---

series of ruptures), as my past breaches surfaces and crosses divides, creating an uncertain future. ('We should recognise that contemporary water is mostly a parody of waters past.' Horn). Perhaps today's dreams are simply yesterday's waters rearranged—a parodic collapsing of past, present and future desires, not turned the right or the wrong way so much as streaming at once through and around me.

fact or fancy,
human being a vacillat
rapidly acquiring the intolerance
For it was this mixture
the obscurity, and granite,
snow;
rudely,
sky good to eat, indeed!
threw a garment like a towel at the naked
unfortunately, fell short by
But let other
haunted by
dilemma. Different though
Suddenly a shadow
risen moon on turbulent
since the world began
lump of sugar
odd, disconnected fragments
violet shadows deepen
not for pay but for Glawr."
natural sympathy which is between the se
tever to alter their identity.
attitudes of great agony
"Life and a lover,"
can be worn indifferently by
A skull;
interspersed with tee-hees and
sex;
in death," Or
completely unwritten. For it is
unwieldy length of this sentence,
soon the whole

Chapter 5

The great cloud which hung
only over this century buffeted, blustering long
consequences beneath its shadow climate.
Girt about with discoloured purples, oranges and reds,
the white of the snow enemies was muddied. Outside,
in unparalleled profusion, no garden lacked a maze—evergreen
rioted in the dank fertility show, innumerable leaves
creaked and glistened. From a damp bonfire
at the end of the earth, rampant cucumbers came scrolloping
and giant cauliflowers disordered the imagination
of special tinted clouds that turned and tumbled
like whales or elephants, a thousand escaping the
whole sky as it spread above
undistinguished gas.

Wind used to spook me—I felt I needed roots. But now at times I can work with the wind—let it ripple my surfaces, carry my limbs. One of my song lyrics once asked in green cascading sound waves, 'Can you convince the wind to change direction?' Having concluded that wind, like trouble, is inevitable, I've learned how best to be in it, like a tree. Are contemporary trees mostly parodies of trees past? I was taught by

Later, extinct monsters cannot even pretend
that the climate was the same puce and flamingo conglomeration
insensibly marbling over other excrescences
—crystal palaces, wedding cakes,
a figure clothed in sponge-bag trousers.
The incongruity of such indecent objects
afflicted Or with the most profound waterlogged air,
a bombazine colour on their cheeks.
Sea-stained, blood-stained,
the manuscript of their poem The Or Tree
had been working for close on three hundred changes—
a gloomy, amorous, satirical
sometimes-drama—fundamentally the same-same brood,
nothing has changed the trees that carp.

---

my English parents to be a gentleman, but the uprightness that involves hasn't always sat comfortably with me—it usually means holding my tongue, binding my limbs, hiding behind trunks. The kind of discipline gentlemen are expected to embody can hinder expression, limit demeanour, confine gender to something rigid, puckered, too particular in its rootedness. In my youth I felt I was able to express myself only

No sooner had thought split than a round-headed monster—
something between a bat and a wombat—
reflected on the eternity of all things infirm,
all of a quiver, all of a stew. Was it damp?
The rain in the ivy could be taken for an answer—
a tingling vibration made of errant fingers playing
the queerest scales (erect themselves).
But remember, we are dealing
with the dankest human soul,
positively ashamed in a strange dress.
What a world we overcome with shame,
that we write not with fingers
but with the hole of a person,
every fibre of our liver trouble completely inclined.

---

through sport and by composing earnest, if wishy-washy, songs, and I did those things well—they grounded me. But occasionally, perhaps out of necessity, I'd bend with the breeze and branch out into other modes, whether or not I knew it on each occasion. Just before I turned 16, with a hot summer underway and my hair at peak opulence, I dressed as an older woman, sweating in makeup and a flowery full-length dress

Or was antipathetic to the man
spirit. As lines bent Or the wrong way,
they dressed lightly in skirts
so as to submit to the new tinglings
of wild autumn winds. Wet as
in Botany Bay, revolving clouds
answered pell-mell
among the violet plumed rain—
'Am single, am mateless, am alone'—
and glanced nervously
lest some mal form flaunting
a long cloak behind them
like a silver pool
came over the birds.

---

as I turned up at the birthday boy's house, a boy who was the most misogynistic in my year. His Liberal-voting mother and the other parents gathered there, sipping their evening cocktails, all thought I was one of them—until they realised I wasn't, that I had tricked them, and this shocked them so much that I could smell the adrenalin as their fight-or-flight instincts kicked in, like I was some sort of animal not to be trusted.

Straight
up into the
golden foam in-
to which the clouds
had churned themselves,
fields of irises fancied then
lowered themselves till they
saw the great hump out at sea
—a nightjar's head pressing lux-
uriously on the love and death suck
of the wet. A few minutes later they became
engaged in the snake-like twisting descent of coming. Un-
important details blew from Or's breakfast to the gilt leopard on the
weathervane: 'You're a woman, you're a man' (since the world began).

Well, obviously—I'm a centaur. Writers have often treated centaurs as liminal beings, slipping as they do between the dual natures they exhibit in myths—the untamed nature they embody in their conflict with the Lapiths (their kin), and the pedagogical nature embodied in teachers like the centaur Chiron. I suppose there's something to ponder in that: should one's trousers be worn on the front legs or the back? There's that

Nowadays, spoonfuls of strawberry jam,
peppermint and the stars
reel overboard,
which is tantamount to saying nothing
—hence the most ordinary
is often the most poetic and the most poetic
is precisely that which cannot be
written, filled to repletion,
a great blank space here, then blobs, lawsuits,
children (they inherit
my sex and shadow—
lolling from their mouths,
cream-coloured ponies command sleep
and snow for pleasure).

---

trouble again, abstracting the self through levity. Yet being neither this nor that, I founder on such singularities: my 'waters exist in monolithic, indivisible continuity with all other waters. No water is separate from any other water' (Horn). Is that why I continue to bottom out here, performing in prose a seriousness that tries to articulate feelings about gender, hoping to offset and underscore the levitating *Choose Your Own*

A parenthesis blazing in the trees
fell fluttering on Or's foot among the azaleas.
A cock entered the current
so as to see the phosphorescence on waves,
icicles clanking,
determined to write all this,
but a thousand other things always echo,
are seductive—
and no single echo was surprised that
a woman could be as ____________ as a man,
and a man as ________ as a woman.
Or rather that both could be so interstranged,
spectre-pale. Shooting this way and that,
Or struck the grass.

Adventure shapes above? Have I founded a duality in these forms? Is duality what I mean by green, or is this, like all writing, some kind of sublimation? I used to retreat into *Choose Your Own Adventure* books as a child—I must've freed a hundred of them from the small, very wooden library in primary school. Their multidirectional construction gave me an illusion of choice that appealed to my imagination's desire

When bright colours like blue and yellow mix themselves
in our eyes, some of it rubs off on our thoughts.
Tossing a little dreamily Or was lying in the bracken
when a leaf cried, 'The wind!' They ran, scattering
Queen Mary's prayer book, snuffing out lights.
They knelt as the shadow came flying, its
growl the word *Obey*, then up they rose
with the lightning and the rain
pouring like wild hawks
till they cr ash ed
and fell in a
sh ow er of fr ag
m en ts to th e
g r o u n d.

---

for liberation within formal structures. Is there an illusion of choice that can free you from entrenched bodily and societal strictures? Would it be a ripple or a disturbance? A wave or a particle? Here's another snippet from a poem amid the leaves: 'I think that the Root of the Wind is Water—' (Emily Dickinson). Could we ground ourselves in that disturbance? We could. Be ripples blown by the wind.

came scrolloping across
overcome with shame,
fact or fancy,
rapidly acquiring
afflicted
For it was this mixture
the obscurity, and granite,
a thousand other things
snake-like twisting
wearing a frock-
since the world began
through all these changes
risen moon on turf
are dealing with
lump of sugar
some strange ecstasy came
THE great cloud which
erect themselves,
violet shadows
pay but for Glawr."
"Life and a lover,"
threw a towel at the naked
natural sympathy which is between the se
as strange and subtle as
discoloured and purples, oranges, and reds
one will only come if it is raining,
can be worn indifferently by
A skull;
evergreen rioted in the damp
unwritten. For it is
length of this sentence,

Chapter 6

Or was completely poem
(anxious matter of getting tingled),
broken off in the middle
of a tribute to eternity,
interrupted with changes, fallen
in love with superstitious reverence
lest it should slip extremely.
But was it marriage was it marriage was it
marriage at the ink pot?
Neck deep in explosion it was dripping
its involuntary pranks again
in purple and dealing
with the most obscure
manifest oceans of the human.

No poem is separate from any other poem. Seeking ways to express gender liberation, fluid and collective, the poem(s) twirling about above exist(s) in monolithic, indivisible continuity with all other poems, while the sentence(s) down here exist(s) in particulate, speculative relation to what's above, and to what's real, biographical, familial. Both flounder in their attempts at representation (like any text), but together perhaps

And so Or now performs a bundle of contraband,
because that's what cures being
a satirist, a cynic, a psychologist.
The transition between writer and subject
is poles asunder—depends on whom
one has lavished so much whim,
this dumb show of emotion, and on whatever
sum this book's publisher may think proper to charge
for this fantasia. Dusk will dusk—
dusk being no better than a corpse,
one of those monsters faithful to poetry—
and which has nothing to do with the subject
of one's autobiographical
petticoat.

---

do something more in their duelling—branching out from, or rippling around, the essential illusion that is oneself. If no self is separate from any other self (I want to believe, have to believe this), my so-called selves must also exist in monolithic, indivisible continuity with all other selves (with F, E, M et al.). Butler writes that 'Styles of various kinds constitute the illusion of an abiding gendered self', whereas acknowledging our

Love, for Or, is slippery—
fluttering purple clouds
passing in the usual cryptic way,
shadow of the starling on the grass, lark
peeping and picking at daisies
the way writers dream
nonsense, snow, moths in green caves, extinction
and the world going on as usual
—an indifferent spectacle.
Human beings are thus gifted
horribly, stuck in the watery,
sometimes fashionable world
(our smutty poem-sort-of-talk
cacophanous).

---

multiple selves or hybrid styles might do away with such illusions, or at least encourage the growth of exploratory roots, renegade branches. And so, if you want to call me they, if you want to describe me as non-binary, or just girly, or if you'd rather call me he (I'm told I look manly in certain lights), I don't mind—I won't straiten your language. ('My Business is Circumference—' Dickinson.) And, in any event, or on whatever side this

Men holding out toys bawl,
women in and out of
spring flowers bawl—
their bodies bawl too.
At some moment of national crisis,
looped and festooned and
ballooned across windows,
statues rebuke The Or Tree,
lampoon now risen
in the age of chocolate
spittoons and hors-d'oeuvres.
A wild experiment. In
degenerate times, writers
Glawr, green some change.

---

needs to go, 'Knowing someone's gender doesn't always tell you much at all about who they are' (Kit Heyam). Likewise, knowing someone's poetry doesn't always tell you much about who they are. ('Power can be defined as the ability to make a particular perspective seem universal.' Vaid-Menon.) Any proclamations made in these passages might seem to be aiming for some peak of universality, but all of them occur in an

Green thought grown plump,
grown sleek, literature is
depressing sex, disillusionment.
Dusk happened. Dusk happens.
Publish instantly! Nothing for it but
to submit to fervent desire.
As it happened a cypher
language invented Or so a
whole state of the utmost
plexity might Glumphoboo
—which summed it up, glancing
at the sky from a boat with a
biscuit in hand and beguiling
their infinitely self-strange works.

---

assemblage of material that offers neither one reading nor another, as any poem can only contain the ashes of its desired form. Just as any poem can only be the surface glint of the life (or lives) glimpsed in its depths. ('Water shines. Water shimmers. Water glows. Water glimmers. Water glitters. Water gleams. Water glistens. Water glints. Water twinkles. Water sparkles. Water blinks. Water winks. Water waves.' Horn.) ('It is

To saw in ignorance, Or's lips began
framing the words into a senseless
singsong of violets, oranges.
Paper got flung, trees spread, art
blurred—pitch bark skirt, alive
and blue-balled, emerald sky.
How scarlet trousers feel was an
extremely uncomfortable feeling. One
must never never bank like somebody
else so manly in the bronze-coloured
waves—a mountain of water, a
glassy death (serpentine,
serpentine,
serpentine).

---

not that one cannot get outside of language in order to grasp materiality in and of itself; rather, every effort to refer to materiality takes place through a signifying process which, in its phenomenality, is always already material. In this sense, then, language and materiality are not opposed, for language both is and refers to that which is material, and what is material never fully escapes from the process by which it is

A golden river coagulated and massed itself
between elephants and whales
of incredible magnitude.
These leviathans get stressed out too.
Their still faces consummate in the street
where we became liquid
—a completely inky book
slipping little ligatures into sonnets.
The conclusion that literature,
since it ate literature,
must be soundproof, must be
of the highest importance ... Nah,
as we have already surpassed our
limit of sonnets, we must omit this.

---

signified.' Butler.) Speaking of signifiers (centaurs), I've been imagining a poem about love, about riding horses together with F, about the binaries each of us relies on to structure existence and make art (left versus right brain, etc.), and about how the body, which is always and already non-binary, can otherwise know exactly what it's doing. Like Orlando's 'The Oak Tree', one can only imagine it—it's amorphous, fictitious—for

Or's conclusion stood looking
as if they had tossed the ball over the net
and must wait for the unseen antagonist to return
its jerky music of the spheres, transport
its waves—or thoughts, which are
of all carriers the best and most clumsy, the most erratic
—over the rooftops and the back gardens
(do you recognise green?). Meanwhile, hail, hail
and bank to bank confounding the Empire,
hail in whatever form it comes!
—and may there be more forms and stranger green
to drown the blue of the vanishing bird dreams,
to tear us asunder, our sleep so deep
that all shapes are ground to dust of infinite softness.

---

now. Perhaps the body of that poem will be written one day, rise from the ashes of a burned book, or flash from the depths of some watery future. ('We cannot accept that water can change, that water can be different, water as the ultimate form of androgyny.' Horn.) We know but never quite accept that trees aren't actually rooted to the spot, that they never stop moving, growing up into the light and down into the dark,

Like a moth, the sky couldn't help
thinking. Thick, watery, prismatic, the clouds
had shrunk—it was a little alarming, this shrinkage.
Everything seemed lit—light poured in until there was a
terrific explosion. It is the present moment. Finally green,
and odd—'I can't even'—Or fell like drops, roundabout
in their ways. Fingering the lit abstractedly, nothing
more quickly disorders it than poetry—the chop-
ping up small of identity which precedes un-
consciousness, a person entirely dis-
assembled. Or will only come
if it is raining, and in
a room of green
curtains.

---

that they send out spores via atmospheric currents, house hundreds of generations of birds, millions of insects, that they're half water and eventually compost themselves back into earth. ('There are so many bridges over [our waters]—it's a virtual forest.' Horn.) There are so many selves between each of us—it's a virtual family. And lest it not go without saying, any piece of ground or body of water sheltered by

Here a
new self came in, a new
self came, in came a new self here,
inside a new self came a self, an in-self came
new in a new here, came skipping over the top
of mind like the beam from a lighthouse—flowering
trees, flowering trees, walk among my flowering trees!
Words like barbaric leaves, haunted, words like nets,
conscious of disseverment, whose fall was so gentle
it had been a smooth green tide. Brooding leaves
were still fluttering thickly. The moon rose over
the world—all was phantom, all was still,
all was lit, like the eggs of some
vast moon-spider.

---

their leaves, or nurtured by their leavings, is confluent with the world at large, including the undulations of subjectivity and identity that animate any particulate sentence. ('Something shimmers, something is hushed up ... what, precisely, in the end, can one say is oneself?' Ashbery.) The flowering of this or that tree, perhaps. The sparkling green of the world's fluidities, writing us into existence.

ecognise the Green
overcome with shame,
came scrolloping
rapidly acquiring
fact or fancy,
precisely the six
risen moon
writing poetry a secret
are dealing with
we quit
Serpentine in this
Violets, oranges,
human bein
snake
dictates of the human heart,
different though
aring a frock-
For it was this mixture
it is the present moment?
the world began
the obscurity,
a thousand other
threw a towel
were inextricably mixed.
sky good to
ecstasy came
THE great cloud which
state of mind
pay but for Glawr.”
natural sympathy which is
the present again struck
shadows and odd
accounts for six or seven selves,
discoloured and purples, oranges, and reds
one will only come if it is raining,
can be worn indifferently by
A skull;
there be more forms, and stranger.
except when the wind is sunk.
For it is
of this sentence,
evergreen rioted

Appendix A

Rewriting the First Sentence of *Orlando*

They—for there could only be doubt about their sex, though the fashion of the time didn't always allow it—was in the act of splicing together their body parts which, like a shattered raft, had been buried by the Muses.

Appendix B
Interview in Or Land

I: Do you exist? Have I made you up?

Or: Tools have their own integrity.

I: I like the unreality of your mind; the whole thing is very splendid and voluptuous and absurd.

Or: I like muddling things up; and if a herb looks nice in a border, then why not grow it there? Why not grow anything anywhere so long as it looks right where it is? That is, surely, the art.

I: I am made and remade continually. Different people draw different words from me.

Or: It is true that you have had infinitely more influence on me intellectually than anyone, and for this alone I love you.

I: My heart currently resembles the ashes of my cigarettes. Is it true that you burned your entire oeuvre?

Or: Autumn in felted slipper shuffles on, muted yet fiery.

I: Flowers really do intoxicate me. You?

Or: Nothing shows up the difference between the things read or said, so much as the daily experience of it.

I: A flowerless room is a soulless room?

Or: To my way of thinking; even a solitary little vase of a living flower may redeem it.

I: I have never more wanted to see you than now.

Or: Not seeing is half-believing.

I: Is it necessary to write, if the days are not to slip emptily by? How else, indeed, to clap the net over the butterfly of the moment?

Or: (That appears to be the suitable formula.) I regret that you have been in bed, though not with me—(a less suitable formula).

I: But listen, suppose Or turns out to be me and it's all about you and the lusts of your flesh and the lure of your mind ... Do you mind, say Yes or No?

Or: No, this is the most delicious, to refuse.

I: Which is the greater ecstacy? The man's or the woman's? And are they not perhaps the same?

Or: It will be recognised that many more people of my type do exist than under the present-day system of hypocrisy is commonly admitted.

I: Need we stress the point?

Or: I contrast my illiterate writing with your scholarly one, and I am ashamed.

I: Like so many knitting needles, purl, plain, purl, plain, achieving a complex pattern of references?

Or: Click, clack, click, clack, goes our conversation.

I: Leopards on the gable-ends? Leopards everywhere?

Or: Yes, you are an agile animal—no doubt about it—but as to your gambols being diverting . . . I'm not so sure . . .

I: Why do you give so much of your energies to the manuscripts of other people? You told me in London that you had at least six novels in your head but were being severe with yourself until you . . .

Or: The liberation of half my personality!

I: Are you a pariah?

Or: [. . .] with a perverse nature? And unnatural feelings?

I: Are you ashamed of duality?

Or: Whom can I lean upon?

I: Too weak and too self-indulgent to struggle?

Or: Authority has every reason to fear the skeptic, for authority can rarely survive in the face of doubt.

I: Had it plucked the rose, or grasped cold steel?

Or: Annihilating myself seemed the only way I could present any type of acceptable self.

I: For the pleasure of being rescued by a green ...

Or: Love?

I: Friendship?

Or: Truth?

I: [...]

Or: I have come to the conclusion, after many years of sad experience, that you cannot come to any conclusion at all.

Notes

'The Or Tree' is largely assembled from burnt fragments of a Vintage Classics edition (published in 2004, on December 2—my birthday) of Virginia Woolf's *Orlando: A Biography* (1928). It was originally drafted for the Centre For Deep Reading's inaugural event 'Woolf Down', January 2017, where a very early version of chapter 6 was performed as part of a talk about the novel.

Before 'The Or Tree' was rewritten as shaped sonnets, an earlier version of chapter 3 was first published in *Rabbit 20: Dance* under a different title, 'The O Tree'; earlier versions of chapters 1 and 2 were published by *Red Room Poetry*; chapter 5 and 'The Or Tree' collages first appeared in *Southerly*'s *Long Paddock*; and chapter 6 was first published in *Rabbit 30: The Long Poem 2*.

'A Note of Explanation, or A Little Introductory Tale of Bemusements and Disenchantment with the Queen' was previously published in *The Chalamet Review* #1, ed. Michael Farrell, 2025. The poem assembles phrases from Vita Sackville-West's *A Note of Explanation: A Little Tale of Secrets and Enchantment from Queen Mary's Dolls' House* (1922).

Despite *Orlando*'s radical gender politics—and for which this book is an homage and could not exist—its first sentence is casually, violently racist, symptomatic of a colonial privilege, as are other moments in the novel. Rather than wash over or ignore this aspect of the original, in 'Appendix A' I've written an alternative, metaphorical opening sentence to invert the violence directed at the decapitated head of an external other by redirecting it toward an internal (and headless) Orphic self.

'Appendix B: Interview in Or Land' cherrypicks questions and phrases from Woolf's *Orlando: A Biography* and Sackville-West's *Selected Writings* and stages them in alternating dialogue.

At the centre of the cover image collage, and subsequent collages surrounding each chapter, is a cut-out of a Romaine Brooks self-portrait, *At the Seaside*, 1914. This is pasted on to a heat map of '/r/place', which was a collaborative and social experiment hosted by *Reddit* on April Fool's Day, 2017. Over those are pasted six layers of fragmented text from a burnt copy of *Orlando: A Biography*, each of the six layers deriving from the novel's six respective chapters. Regarding *At the Seaside*, one day while researching *Orlando* I took a deep dive on Google Images into cover art for the novel and came across this portrait gracing the front of a Spanish edition—I was struck by the subject of the painting's likeness to a younger version of myself.

Acknowledgements

To Frances, whose unwavering heart gives me courage; to Evie and Matilda, whose love is as natural and fluid as their sense of gender; and to River, born too recently to enter this book; and to mum and dad and my brother—I love you all. I'd also like to thank Chris Edwards for years of incisive and caring editorial feedback on the many lives and selves of the manuscript, and Rae White for their sensitivity reading and encouraging feedback. Thanks, finally, to Upswell for turning my vision into reality; to Terri-ann, Becky, Kelly and Keith for all the labour that went into producing this book.

Bibliography

Travis Alabanza, 'The Sea', *Out Magazine*, 2017.

Travis Alabanza, *None of the Above: Reflections on Life Beyond the Binary*, 2022.

John Ashbery, *Girls on the Run*, 1999.

John Ashbery, 'This Room', *Your Name Here*, 2000.

Julie L Belcove, 'Roni Horn', *W Magazine*, 2009.

Giovanni Boccaccio, *The Decameron*, 1353, trans. G H McWilliam, 2003.

Kate Bornstein, *Gender Outlaw: On Men, Women, and the Rest of Us*, 1994.

Romaine Brooks, *Strange Impressions*, 2022.

Judith Butler, *Bodies that Matter: On the Discursive Limits of 'Sex'*, 1993.

Judith Butler, *Gender Trouble: Feminism and the Subversion of Identity*, 1990.

Judith Butler, *Giving an Account of Oneself*, 2003.

Hélène Cixous, 'Portraits of Portraits: The Very Day/Light of Roni Horn', in Roni Horn, *A Kind of You: 6 Portraits*, 2007.

Samuel Taylor Coleridge, 'Dejection: An Ode', 1802.

Lydia Davis, 'Form as a Response to Doubt', in Mary Burger (ed.), *Biting the Error: Writers Explore Narrative*, 2004.

Emily Dickinson, poem no. 1302, 1874; letter to her editor, 1862.

Leslie Feinberg, *Stone Butch Blues*, 1993.

Toby Fitch, 'All the Skies Above *Girls on the Run*' and 'Often I Am Permutated into a Mermaid', *Where Only the Sky had Hung Before*, 2019.

T Fleischmann, *Time is the Thing a Body Moves Through*, 2019.

Vanessa Guignery and Wojciech Drag, *The Poetics of Fragmentation in Contemporary British and American Fiction*, 2019.

Kit Heyam, *Before We Were Trans: A New History of Gender*, 2022.

Roni Horn, *Another Water*, 2000.

Roni Horn, interview with Claudia Spinelli, *Journal of Contemporary Art*, 1995.

Roni Horn, *Roni Horn Aka Roni Horn*, 2009.

James Joyce, *Finnegan's Wake*, 1939.

Vladimir Mayakovsky, 'A Cloud in Trousers', 1915, trans. P Lemke, *Russian Poetry: The Modern Period*, 1978.

Maggie Nelson, interview with Ben Segal, *Continent*, 2011.

Frank O'Hara, 'Autobiographia Literaria' and 'Poem' ('Green things are flowers too'), *Collected Poems*, 1967.

Vita Sackville-West, *A Note of Explanation: A Little Tale of Secrets and Enchantment from Queen Mary's Dolls' House*, 1922, 2017.

Vita Sackville-West, *Vita Sackville-West: Selected Writings*, 2015.

William Shakespeare, *Hamlet*, c. 1599–1601.

Alok Vaid-Menon, *Beyond the Gender Binary*, 2020.

McKenzie Wark, 'A New Kind of Trans Poetics', *The Nation*, 2022.

McKenzie Wark, 'Paper Princess', *Sydney Review of Books*, 2020.

Virginia Woolf, 'The Modern Essay', 1925.

Virginia Woolf, *Orlando: A Biography*, 1928.

About Upswell

Upswell Publishing was established in 2021 by Terri-ann White as a not-for-profit press. A perceived gap in the market for distinctive literary works in fiction, poetry and narrative non-fiction was the motivation. In her years as a bookseller, writer and then publisher, Terri-ann has maintained a watch on literary books and the way they insinuate themselves into a cultural space and are then located within our literary and cultural inheritance. She is interested in making books to last: books with the potential to still be noticed, and noted, after decades and thus be ripe to influence new literary histories.

About this typeface

Book designer Becky Chilcott chose Foundry Origin not only as a strong, carefully considered, and dependable typeface, but also to honour her late friend and mentor, type designer Freda Sack, who oversaw the project. Designed by Freda's long-standing colleague, Stuart de Rozario, much like Upswell Publishing, Foundry Origin was created out of the desire to say something new.